T0253008

The Parable of

THE HAND AND THE GLOVE:

A Spiritual Awakening

ALLEN SMITHSON

abbott press®

A DIVISION OF WRITER'S DIGEST

THE PARABLE OF THE HAND AND THE GLOVE:
A SPIRITUAL AWAKENING

Abbott Press books may be ordered through booksellers or by contacting:

Abbott Press
1663 Liberty Drive
Bloomington, IN 47403
www.abbottpress.com
Phone: 1-866-697-5310

ISBN: 978-1-4582-0195-9 (e)
ISBN: 978-1-4582-0194-2 (sc)

Library of Congress Control Number: 2012901852

Printed in the United States of America

Abbott Press rev. date: 3/14/2012

Each time you wear gloves or look at your hands, remember this little story.

Once there was a beautiful peaceful, forgiving, divine, HAND that had deep gratitude, love, and compassion for everyone. It was grateful for others and circumstances just as they were. It had oodles of energy which it used to bless everyone. It interacted enthusiastically with other hands without negative judgment. Its communications were always uplifting. It went about completing tasks with two goals. Its foremost intention and top priority was to act WITH awareness, and compassion toward others. Its secondary purpose was to accomplish the task "at hand".

Shortly this hand noticed that all hands had gloves on all of the time. It noticed that IT was wearing a glove as well.

As it went about, it noticed all shapes, colors, and kinds of gloves. Some gloves were designed for manual labor. Other gloves had specific purposes; Daddy gloves, Mommy gloves, brother and sister gloves, and so forth. Many gloves were specially designed for a particular occupation: Attorney gloves, doctor, banker, athlete, insurance agent, salesman, student, teacher, prisoner and prison keeper gloves.

Every task had a different glove. Some were made for protection. There were even gloves for hurting others.

Since no one ever saw the hands which were inside, it was difficult to distinguish between the hand and the glove. Soon it forgot that all the gloves it saw had hands inside.

The hand went around thinking IT WAS a glove. After all, a glove was the only thing it could see in the mirror. All of its memories were of being one glove or another. Whenever it thought about itself, it thought about the glove's qualities. All of its value seemed to come from the gloves it wore.

Little if any benefit seemed to come from the hand. Only a feeling or idea here and there came from the hand and it was questionable whether the prompting was for the GLOVE'S best good.

Some even said that hands didn't actually exist. They taught that hands were just figments of the imagination.

The hand, which now thought that it was a glove looked around and mused, "I want to be like that glove over there. It has rubies and diamonds, drives a nice car, and holds the latest smart phone." Or, "I want to be like that one over there, it can DO more in an hour than I do in a day."

With practice, the hand could easily switch between many different gloves. It had a glove for home, another for work, one for sports, another for getting power, one for experiencing pain, another for inflicting pain, one for arguing, and another for church.

As it turns out, it could instantly "PUT ON" a glove for pretty much any situation.

As a glove, it wanted everyone's approval, and it was quite concerned with what folks thought. In fact, when choosing which glove to PUT ON, it gave more credence to what it thought others wanted to see than to what it wanted to be. Much of its conduct was dictated by the society in which it lived.

Possibly related to this need for approval, it nursed a lot of feelings of shame and guilt about the past.

It had compelling opinions on many subjects which it freely expressed in order to persuade others to agree with it. The more everyone agreed with it, the more entrenched the opinion became. The glove loved being RIGHT! It liked being right more than it liked being at peace.

As a glove it felt smarter and better. It wanted to do things, "My Way!" not realizing that "MY WAY" was actually the way of the glove not the hand. It liked thrills and having control over others.

It had numerous expectations and spent a lot of energy WANTING things to be the way they "SHOULD" be. Sometimes when its expectations were not met, it became angry.

Within the boundaries of society, it enjoyed being DIFFERENT from other gloves. Gloves compared themselves with each other constantly. After all, the glove's nature is to help the hand function in a different way.

Since there was always some other glove that was better at a task, or had better stuff, had more value, or was getting more attention, the glove often felt ashamed, worthless, misunderstood, insecure, unsafe, envious, anxious, sad, fearful, or just plain uneasy.

It frequently felt picked on. It was often CRITICAL or fearful of others. It occasionally told them how unfairly it was being treated.

No matter what glove it was wearing, it wanted MORE! SO, it went about SEEKING acceptance, value, happiness, pleasure, thrills, control over others, and joy.

It searched for happiness by getting better stuff than others. It would DO anything to get nicer possessions, greater security, higher status, and more attention.

As a glove, the hand was 100% sure that happiness was just around the next corner. But whenever it got more attention, and with every new acquisition, the satisfaction didn't last long at all! There was always something missing. It wanted MORE! And watch out if it didn't get more … right now! The long lasting fulfillment and satisfaction it sought were repeatedly illusive, but it just kept insanely trying to find happiness in the same old way.

It didn't understand the purpose of circumstances. It made circumstances part of its glove identity. It "owned" the circumstance it was in. It owned "MY" possession, "MY" talent, "My" personality, "My" technique, and "My" favorite. As strange as it may seem, it complained about and fought against many of the circumstances IT had blended with its glove self. It spent loads of time, energy and money trying to get rid of "MY" troubles, "MY" habit, "MY" problem, "MY" fear, "MY" disease, "MY" shame, and "MY" pain.

The glove had a lot of troubles. It BELIEVED that the CAUSE of its unhappiness and distress was someone else, or some organization, or a painful circumstance, or lack of possessions.

One day it felt a stirring inside. It turned its attention inward. It took the time to STOP be still, observe, ask, and listen. "Were hands an illusion, or was it gloves that were an illusion? Were gloves permanent and authentic? It experienced waves of illuminating INsight. The truth became bright clear and in focus, asserting a fact that could not be denied.

"I AM A HAND NOT A GLOVE!"

Wow! What an epiphany! The true cause of all its distress had been the persistent but mistaken belief that it WAS the glove it had on.

The experience was a little bit like waking up. It felt creative, alert, and more alive than ever before. It had HOPE based on inner perception. It found itself on a new path enlightened by the awareness of its essence. The happiness it franticly pursued before now seemed to emanate effortlessly from inside.

It REALized that the life, the VALUE, and the magic which makes all gloves move-and come to being is the hand. All REAL value came from the hand. It REALized that energy, power, peace, fulfillment, and joy came from inside itself. It began to live LIFE to its fullest.

It now perceived itself and other HANDS, separately from the gloves they were wearing. It noticed that gloves had many important functions. For example, it noticed that when gloves shared a loving embrace it allowed the hands to communicate in a way that was apparently impossible without the glove.

It observed circumstances and LEARNED FROM THEM without labeling, judging, or identifying with them.

Although it could not be totally gloveless certain EXPERIENCES allowed it to pull back the glove a little and peek at the hand inside.

Any action that increased self-control gave the hand more influence than the glove. Genuine acts of selfless service made the hand shine right through.

It practiced OBSERVING gloves and hands for what they were without getting into the drama. It experienced enormous waves of deep unconditional love for others.

It began thinking more hand thoughts than glove thoughts, giving it a new perspective on reality. It pretty much knew how gloves were made, but how were hands made? Where did THEY come from?

It learned to ask its Creator questions and it practiced actively paying attention to, and following, the INTO-IT-ive promptings of ITs inner hand.

Changing gloves provided an opportunity to see its hand so long as it noticed itself changing rather than being caught up in the turbulence of the situation.

Just as the glove couldn't talk and listen at the same time, it knew that its hand could not listen to its creator amidst constant mind chatter. In STILL QUIET meditative moments it silenced the relentless glove-mind chatter and noticed itself AS a hand inside of a glove. The delusion that it was a glove continued to fade away.

It began to give "NOW" its full attention rather than getting caught up in the emotional drama of the past and future. As it turned out, "Now" was an amazingly delightful place and time to live.

It recognized all others as the genuine brothers and sisters that they were. It had a special unseen bond and connection to others that were in the process of realizing they were hands. The fact that everyone without exception could experience this realization and enjoy free flowing happiness became clear.

It REALized the fact of nature that, unlike hands, all gloves will eventually be taken off and discarded.

With this epiphany came the logical understanding that the glove was the ONLY thing that anyone else could harm.

No one could upset the hand by stealing from it. No one could offend it by ignoring or demeaning it. Even glove on glove assaults couldn't injure it. No one could "lay a glove on it!"

There was no bona fide need to defend itself or feel FEAR. It now had the courage to entertain a vision of fresh new possibilities. It was amazed at the extent to which fear had restricted love in its life.

Once the hand knew from experience that it was a divine hand inside of a glove it was no longer caught up in the fearful struggle for security, attention, and getting better stuff than its peers.

It IN-VISION-ed itself and others quite differently now. IT SAW RIGHT THROUGH the gloves being worn including its own, no matter how thick or abused, no matter how old and tattered, no matter how misguided or intimidating, no matter the occupation, no matter the intensity of emotion being expressed. It just noticed splendid beautiful hands.

Perceiving other's hands instead of their gloves somehow helped others recognize their own immortal hand.

With this new INsight it returned to being a peaceful, forgiving, divine HAND with a deep sense of gratitude, love, and compassion for everyone. It was grateful for others and circumstances just as they were. It once again had oodles of energy that it used for blessing everyone. It interacted enthusiastically with other hands without negative judgment. Its communications were always INspiring.

The hand went about completing tasks with two goals. Its foremost intention and top priority was to act WITH awareness, and compassion toward others. Its SECONDARY purpose was to accomplish the task "at hand".

1 Cor. 2:14 "But the natural man receiveth not the things of God: for they are foolishness unto him: neither can he know them because they are spiritually discerned."

1 John 3:1-3: Behold, what manner of love the Father hath bestowed upon us, that we should be called the sons of God: therefore the world knoweth us not because it knew him not. Beloved, now are we the sons of God, and IT DOTH NOT YET APPEAR WHAT WE SHALL BE: but we know that, when he shall appear, we shall be like him; for we shall see him as he is. And every man that hath this HOPE in him purifieth himself, even as he is pure.

Luke 17: 20-21 And when he was demanded of the Pharisees, when the kingdom of God should come, he answered them and said, The kingdom of God cometh not with observation: Neither shall they say, Lo here! Or, lo there! For, behold the kingdom of God is WITHIN YOU.